GRAMMATICAL AIDS

FOR

STUDENTS

OF

NEW TESTAMENT GREEK

Grammatical Aids

FOR

STUDENTS OF

NEW TESTAMENT GREEK

By

Walter Mueller

WILLIAM B. EERDMANS PUBLISHING COMPANY
GRAND RAPIDS, MICHIGAN

Copyright © 1972 by William B. Eerdmans Publishing Company
All rights reserved
Library of Congress Catalog Card Number: 74-184695
ISBN 0-8028-1447-6

Third printing, September 1977

To Janet, the woman

behind the man

Printed in the United States of America

FOREWORD

I am happy to have the opportunity of writing a brief foreword in commendation of this useful handbook. It would be difficult to overstress the importance of a thorough knowledge of the grammatical forms of the Greek language as the indispensable basis for a sound and intelligent exegesis of the Greek New Testament. The man whose knowledge of grammar is unreliable is bound to be unreliable in his exegesis also. For too long too many congregations have suffered from the pretentious incompetence of preachers who hope to impress their hearers by referring with assumed erudition to the 'original Greek' from the unassailable stronghold of the pulpit. The regrettable fact is that today the majority of seminarians are thrust into exegesis classes with no more Greek than they have been able to retain from the few weeks of a summer 'crash' course. It is hardly surprising that the manner of their intake of the language has left them suffering from both undernourishment and indigestion, and that for so many this proves to be an incurable affliction.

This small volume which sets out clearly and without frills the basic essentials of New Testament Greek in its grammatical and nonsyntactic structures has a role to play in stemming the present decline. It provides a means whereby the student of the language of the New Testament can help himself. What he must do, quite simply, is to learn the forms given in the following pages until he knows them by heart and they come naturally to him. To do this is not at all a superhuman task, nor need it be a joyless chore — in the process of memorization means can be devised of pleasantly competing with oneself. And the person who does this will know, to his lasting benefit and gratification, that he is equipping himself to become a sensible and effective expositor of the sacred text. He will be grateful, too, that Mr. Mueller's enthusiasm for the language and his eagerness to encourage others in its study have caused him to undertake the labor of preparing so serviceable a handbook.

—PHILIP EDGCUMBE HUGHES

PREFACE

This work is intended to be nothing more than its title indicates. It is not a substitute for a complete New Testament Greek Grammar. Indeed, to be used properly it must be used with a standard grammar. It is not meant to provide a "short cut" method to a mastery of Greek grammar, for there is none. Greek grammar can be mastered only by hard work and concentration. These aids will be useful only to those who already have, or are in the process of gaining, a basic knowledge of the principles of New Testament Greek grammar.

The charts and text constituting this work are simply *Grammatical Aids for Students of New Testament Greek.* As aids they have various purposes.

1. They are meant to assist the student in seeing the logical relationships between the various forms of the most important parts of speech included in the study of New Testament Greek.

2. A second purpose is closely related to the first. When the student sees the logical relationships that exist, his work load is lightened, since memorization is then reduced to a minimum. Rather than memorizing hundreds of different forms the student will commit to memory certain basic forms. In addition to these basic forms he need then memorize only those principles which are necessary to construct other related forms, plus the exceptions to those principles and forms where they exist.

   The most obvious illustration of this is in the relationship between the conjugation of the present indicative active and that of the future indicative active. Both conjugations are the same with the exception of the presence of the σ following the verb stem and before the personal endings in the future. If the student memorizes the present endings and the principle that the sign of the future is σ, he has learned two conjugations in the time it normally takes to learn one.

3. A final purpose of this work is to provide a practical aid for those students who have already taken elementary Greek but who find themselves in the position of needing a simplified reference work to assist them in further study. The persons who fit into this category are students who are engaged in courses in advanced Greek or exegesis, ministers who

wisely see the need of utilizing their knowledge of Greek in independent study and sermon preparation, and any others who, for various reasons, need to refer to the New Testament in its original language.

I express my sincere thanks to Dr. Philip Edgcumbe Hughes, my friend and colleague, for writing the foreword to this book, to Dr. Bruce M. Metzger for reading the manuscript and making various suggestions, and to Miss Marilyn Olsen, my former secretary, for typing the English portions of the original manuscript.

I wish also to thank those who were my seminary students in New Testament Greek for providing me with the needed impetus to prepare this book, which I had long before recognized as necessary.

WALTER MUELLER

CONTENTS

I. ACCENT

ACCENT

I. General Rules

1. Only the last three syllables of a Greek word may be accented.
    a. The last syllable is known as the ULTIMA.
    b. The next to last is called the PENULT.
    c. The syllable before the penult is known as the ANTEPENULT.

2. There are 3 types of accents
    a. **ACUTE** (′)
        1) May be placed on any of the last three syllables.
        2) May be placed on the antepenult only if the ultima is short.
        3) When found on the ultima with other words following, without intervening punctuation, it will change to a grave.

    b. **CIRCUMFLEX** (˜)
        1) May be placed only on the penult or ultima.
        2) May be placed only on a long syllable.
        3) May be placed on the penult only if the ultima is short (αι or οι are considered short when used in the ultima *without* another letter following).

    c. **GRAVE** (ˋ)
        1) May be placed only on the ultima.
        2) Words must follow without intervening punctuation.

These rules may be visualized as in the accompanying chart.

	ANTEPENULT	PENULT	ULTIMA
ACUTE ′	′ (only when ultima is short)	′	′ (changes to a grave if followed by another word)
CIRCUMFLEX ˜ (only on long syllables)		˜ (only when ultima is short)	˜
GRAVE ˋ (only when words follow without intervening punctuation)			ˋ

3. If the PENULT is to be accented
   and the penult is LONG
   and the ULTIMA is SHORT
   then the PENULT will be accented with a CIRCUMFLEX.

II. Rules for Accenting Nouns

1. The position of the accent in the nominative singular must be learned from the lexicon. The other cases will accent the same syllable as the nominative if the last syllable permits. If the last syllable will not permit the same syllable to be accented the accent will fall on the following syllable.

2. In the genitive and dative cases, both singular and plural, a long ultima, if accented, will take a circumflex.

III. Rules for Accenting Verbs

There is only one rule for verb accent in addition to the general rules already noted.

The accent of a verb is recessive. That is, it is placed on the antepenult or as close to the antepenult as the rules will allow.

IV. Exceptions to the Accent Rules

1. There are some specific exceptions to the rules previously stated which must be committed to memory as they are encountered.

2. There are also two general exceptions:
   a. A PROCLITIC is a word so closely related to the word that follows it as to have no accent of its own.
   b. An ENCLITIC is a word so closely related to the word that precedes it as to have no accent of its own.

II. NOUNS

NOUNS

A. FIRST OR A DECLENSION

General Rule for Accenting a Declension Nouns

In the a declension the genitive plural will invariably be accented with a circumflex on the ultima.

LONG a TYPE	η TYPE
χώρα – "country"	σκηνή – "tent"
S. N. χώρ α	S. N. σκην ή
G. χώρ ας	G. σκην ῆς
D. χώρ ᾳ	D. σκην ῇ
A. χώρ αν	A. σκην ήν
P. N. χῶρ αι	P. N. σκην αί
G. χωρ ῶν	G. σκην ῶν
D. χώρ αις	D. σκην αῖς
A. χώρ ας	A. σκην άς
1. ε, ι, or ρ must precede the ending. 2. Nouns of this type are feminine.	1. If ε, ι, or ρ do not precede the endings, the singular forms will have η in place of a. 2. Nouns of this type are feminine.

NOTE: Because of the infrequency of its use in the New Testament, the vocative case is omitted throughout in the treatment of nouns. It is sufficient to say that the vocative generally assumes the same form as the nominative. A general exception to this is that the vocative singular of second declension nouns of the masculine variety (ος type) is formed by adding an ε to the noun stem. Thus the vocative of κύριος is κύριε.

SHORT α TYPE

ἀλήθεια – "truth"

	S.	N.	ἀλήθει α	P.	N.	ἀλήθει αι
		G.	ἀληθεί ας		G.	ἀληθει ῶν
		D.	ἀληθεί ᾳ		D.	ἀληθεί αις
		A.	ἀλήθει αν		A.	ἀληθεί ας

1. The endings are exactly the same as those of the long α type.

2. The short α appears only in the nominative and accusative singular forms. Thus the change in accent position.

3. This type, like the long α type, may have an ε, ι, or ρ preceding the ending. In this particular word the type is recognized by the position of the accent in the nominative singular.

4. Nouns of this type are feminine.

ας TYPE

νεανίας – "young man"

	S.	N.	νεανί ας	P.	N.	νεανί αι
		G.	νεανί ου		G.	νεανι ῶν
		D.	νεανί ᾳ		D.	νεανί αις
		A.	νεανί αν		A.	νεανί ας

1. Since the endings are preceded by ε, ι, or ρ, α will appear in the endings of the nominative, dative, and accusative singular forms.

2. The nominative singular form ends in ας, hence the name "ας Type." The genitive singular will end in ου. Elsewhere the endings of the long α type will be found.

3. Nouns of this type are masculine.

ης TYPE

μαθητής – "disciple"

	S.	N.	μαθητ ής	P.	N.	μαθητ αί
		G.	μαθητ οῦ		G.	μαθητ ῶν
		D.	μαθητ ῇ		D.	μαθητ αῖς
		A.	μαθητ ήν		A.	μαθητ άς

1. Since the ending is not preceded by an ε, ι, or ρ, η will appear in the nominative, dative, and accusative singular forms.

2. The nominative singular ends in ης. Like the ας type the genitive singular will end in ου. Elsewhere the endings of the η type will be found.

3. Nouns of this type are masculine.

B. SECOND OR O DECLENSION

General Rule for Accenting o Declension Nouns

In the o declension the genitive and dative cases, both singular and plural, when accented on the ultima are accented with a circumflex.

ος TYPE

λόγος — "word"

S.	N. λόγ ος	P.	N. λόγ οι	1.	This type receives its name from the ος ending of the nominative singular.
	G. λόγ ου		G. λόγ ων		
	D. λόγ ῳ		D. λόγ οις	2.	Nouns of this type are masculine.
	A. λόγ ον		A. λόγ ους		

ον TYPE

δῶρον — "gift"

S.	N. δῶρ ον	P.	N. δῶρ α	1.	This type receives its name from the ον ending of the nominative singular.
	G. δώρ ου		G. δώρ ων		
	D. δώρ ῳ		D. δώρ οις	2.	Nouns of this type are neuter.
	A. δῶρ ον		A. δῶρ α		

C. THIRD OR CONSONANT DECLENSION

General Observations

1. The various types of this declension receive their names on the basis of the final letter or letters of the noun stem.

2. The stems of the consonant declension nouns are not evident in the nominative singular forms. The stems of nouns in this declension are usually found in the genitive singular.

3. The basic endings (see below) should be mastered first. These endings are then added to the stem according to fairly well-defined rules.

4. If the stem of a consonant declension noun is monosyllabic, the genitive and dative cases, both singular and plural, will be accented on the ultima.

19

Basic Consonant Declension Endings

		Masculine and Feminine	Neuter
S.	N.	ς	—
	G.	ος	ος
	D.	ι	ι
	A.	α	—
P.	N.	ες	α
	G.	ων	ων
	D.	σι	σι
	A.	ας	α

All of the above endings are short with the exception of the genitive plural.

MUTE TYPE

Masculine	Neuter
σάρξ — "flesh"	ὄνομα — "name"

S. N. σάρ ξ   P. N. σάρκ ες

G. σαρκ ός   G. σαρκ ῶν

D. σαρκ ί   D. σαρ ξί

A. σάρκ ι   A. σάρκ ας

The mute joins with a σ in the nominative singular and dative plural. As a result a contraction takes place according to the following pattern:

$$\pi, \beta, \phi + \sigma = \psi$$

$$\kappa, \gamma, \chi + \sigma = \xi$$

$$\tau, \delta, \theta + \sigma = \sigma$$

S. N. ὄνομα *

G. ὀνόματ ος

D. ὀνόματ ι

A. ὄνομα *

P. N. ὀνόματ α

G. ὀνομάτ ων

D. ὀνόμα σι

A. ὀνόματ α

* The τ of the stem is dropped since τ cannot stand as the final letter of a word.

	S.	N.	ποιμήν		P.	N.	ποιμέν ες
LIQUID TYPE		G.	ποιμέν ος			G.	ποιμέν ων
ποιμήν —"shepherd"		D.	ποιμέν ι			D.	ποιμέ σι
		A.	ποιμέν α			A.	ποιμέν ας

1. The liquid consonants are λ, μ, ν, and ρ. The majority of words of this type have stems endings in ν or ρ.
2. In the nominative singular the liquid consonant rejects the ς ending and the preceding vowel of the stem is lengthened if it is not already long.
3. In the dative plural of words whose stems end in ν, the ν is dropped before the σ of the case ending.

SYNCOPATED LIQUID TYPE

πατήρ – "father"

S.	N.	πατήρ	P.	N.	πατέρ ες
	G.	πατρ ός (πατέρ + ος)		G.	πατέρ ων
	D.	πατρ ί (πατέρ + ι)		D.	πατρά σι (πατερ + ά + σι)
	A.	πατέρ α		A.	πατέρ ας

1. This type is referred to as the syncopated liquid type because syncope (the dropping of a short vowel between two consonants) takes place in the genitive and dative singular and in the dative plural. In the dative plural an α is inserted following the liquid consonant and before the case ending.
2. Otherwise this type is similar to the liquid type.
3. Many irregularities occur in nouns of this type. These irregularities should be learned by consulting a lexicon.

ς TYPE

κρέας —"meat"

S.	N.	κρέα ς	P.	N.	κρέα (κρέα + α)
	G.	κρέ ως (κρέα + ος)		G.	κρε ῶν (κρεά + ων)
	D.	κρέα ι (κρέα + ι)		D.	κρέα σι
	A.	κρέα ς		A.	κρέα

1. The final ς is dropped in all cases except the nominative and accusative singular.
2. The final vowel of the noun stem, in those cases where the ς is dropped, is contracted with the vowel of the case ending according to the rules of contraction for contract verbs. See pp. 39f.
3. When two vowels come together which could form a diphthong, a diphthong is formed. For example, ε + ι = ει and α + ι = αι.
4. In nouns that have an ε as the final vowel of the stem, the ε is changed to ο in the nominative and accusative singular.

21

VOWEL TYPES

ι Stem	υ Stem
πόλις — "city"	ἰχθύς — "fish"
S. N. πόλι ς	S. N. ἰχθύ ς
* G. πόλε ως	G. ἰχθύ ος
D. πόλε ι	D. ἰχθύ ι
A. πόλι ν	A. ἰχθύ ν
P. N. πόλε ις	P. N. ἰχθύ ες
* G. πόλε ων	G. ἰχθύ ων
D. πόλε σι	D. ἰχθύ σι
A. πόλε ις	* A. ἰχθῦ ς

* These accents are an exception to the rules for accenting.	* The accent is a circumflex to compensate for the dropping of the α and because it is a long, essentially contracted syllable.

1. Words with an ι stem retain the ι only in the nominative and accusative singular. Elsewhere the ι is changed to ε. This same phenomenon occurs in *some* words with a υ stem.

2. In several cases contraction does *not* occur in accordance with the regular rules of contraction.

   a. In the genitive singular of the ι stem nouns the ο is changed to an ω and remains uncontracted. In the υ stem nouns the ο is retained and no contraction takes place.

   b. In the accusative singular the regular α ending is dropped and is replaced by a ν.

   c. In the genitive plural no contraction takes place. An uncontracted form is retained.

   d. In the accusative plural of the ι stem nouns the ending is εις; in the υ stem nouns the α is dropped leaving the ending υς.

DIPHTHONG TYPE

βασιλεύς — "king"

S.	N.	*βασιλεύ*	*ς*
	G.	*βασιλέ*	*ως*
	D.	*βασιλεῖ*	
	A.	*βασιλέ*	*α*
P.	N.	*βασιλεῖ*	*ς*
	G.	*βασιλέ*	*ων*
	D.	*βασιλεῦ*	*σι*
	A.	*βασιλεῖ*	*ς*

1. The diphthong will have *υ* as its final letter.

2. When the case ending begins with a consonant (nominative singular and dative plural) the *υ* will remain and join the case ending without a contraction taking place.

3. When the ending begins with a vowel the *υ* is dropped and the following should be noted:

   a. In the dative singular and nominative plural contraction will take place as expected.

   b. In other cases irregularities occur which are too numerous to note.

III. VERBS

VERBS

A. CONSTRUCTION OF VERBS

The basic principle to be remembered in the study of Greek verb forms is that verbs are "built" or "constructed."

This principle is adhered to throughout the charts that follow. In the charts the various parts of the construction are separated from each other.

Thus, ἐλελύκεμεν is shown as ἐ λε λύ κ εμεν. (The parts of the verb in the order in which they are shown are, augment, reduplication, stem, sign of the perfect, and personal ending.)

The stem is the foundation of any verb. This must be found before a verb may be constructed.

To the stem the following are added as they are necessary:

1. *Personal Endings* — every conjugation of the verb will have its own personal endings.

   In the *active voice* these endings will *vary* from tense to tense.

   In the *middle voice*, and in *all passives but the future and aorist*, endings are determined by whether the tense is primary or secondary.

   Primary tense (Present, Future, Perfect) endings are:

S.	1.	μαι	P.	1.	μεθα
	2.	σαι		2.	σθε
	3.	ται		3.	νται

   Secondary tense (Imperfect, Aorist, Pluperfect) endings are:

S.	1.	μην	P.	1.	μεθα
	2.	σο		2.	σθε
	3.	το		3.	ντο

   The future and aorist tenses in the passive voice have their own characteristic endings.

27

2. *Augment* — will be found only in the secondary tenses in the indicative mood. Augment is of two kinds:

   a. Syllabic — verbs beginning with a consonant are augmented by prefixing an ϵ to the verb stem.

   b. Temporal — verbs beginning with a vowel are augmented by lengthening that vowel.

$$a \text{ and } \epsilon \text{ become } \eta$$
$$\breve{\iota}, \ o \text{ and } \breve{\upsilon} \text{ become } \bar{\iota}, \omega, \bar{\upsilon}$$
$$\alpha\iota \text{ and } \alpha \text{ become } \eta$$
$$\omicron\iota \text{ becomes } \omega$$

3. *Reduplication* — this phenomenon appears regularly in the perfect tenses and elsewhere in certain irregular verbs. Reduplication occurs according to the following pattern:

   a. When the verb begins with a consonant the initial letter is repeated followed by an ϵ. If the initial consonant is a rough mute (θ, χ, ϕ) the cognate smooth form (τ, κ, π) is used in the reduplication.

   b. Verbs beginning with a vowel reduplicate with a temporal augment.

   c. Verbs beginning with two or more consonants, or one of the double consonants (ζ, ξ, ψ, ρ), reduplicate by means of a syllabic augment.

4. *Tense and Voice Signs*

   a. σ is the sign of the future tense.

   b. $\sigma\alpha$ is the sign of the aorist tense.

   c. κ is the sign of the perfect and the pluperfect tenses (in the active voice only).

   d. $\theta\eta$ is the sign of the passive voice.

5. *Connecting Vowels* — where used, these will precede the personal endings.

   a. o is used before μ and ν.

   b. ϵ is used elsewhere.

> Note: Due to the infrequent use of the optative mood in the New Testament it has been omitted from this work.

B. THE Ω CONJUGATION

λύω – "loose"

1. THE INDICATIVE MOOD

These forms, as well as the general rules for verb formation, should be mastered by the student. The various forms in all other moods will be mastered by comparison and contrast with these.

PRESENT

Active				*Middle and Passive*			
S. 1. λύ ω	P. 1. λύ ομεν			S. 1. λύ ο μαι	P. 1. λυ ό μεθα		
2. λύ εις	2. λύ ετε			2. λύ ῃ	2. λύ ε σθε		
3. λύ ει	3. λύ ουσι			3. λύ ε ται	3. λύ ο νται		

FUTURE

Active

S. 1. λύ σ ω	P. 1. λύ σ ομεν	These forms are exactly the same as those of the present tense except for the σ (sign of the future) which is added to the verb stem.
2. λύ σ εις	2. λύ σ ετε	
3. λύ σ ει	3. λύ σ ουσι	

Middle

S. 1. λύ σ ο μαι	P. 1. λυ σ ό μεθα	indicative middle and passive except for the σ (sign of the future) which is added to the verb stem.
2. λύ σ ῃ	2. λύ σ ε σθε	
3. λύ σ ε ται	3. λύ σ ο νται	

1. These forms are exactly the same as those of the present

2. It should be remembered that the future, unlike the present, has separate conjugations for the middle and passive voices.

Passive

S. 1. λυ θή σ ο μαι	P. 1. λυ θη σ ό μεθα	These forms are exactly the same as the future indicative middle except for the θη combination (sign of the passive) which is added to the stem *before* the σ (sign of the future).
2. λυ θή σ ῃ	2. λυ θή σ ε σθε	
3. λυ θή σ ε ται	3. λυ θή σ ο νται	

IMPERFECT

Active

S. 1. ἔ λυ ον   P. 1. ἐ λύ ομεν

   2. ἔ λυ ες   2. ἐ λύ ετε

   3. ἔ λυ ε   3. ἔ λυ ον

The augment (ε) is prefixed to the verb stem since this is a secondary tense. This is also true of the middle and passive forms below.

Middle and Passive

S. 1. ἐ λυ ό μην   P. 1. ἐ λυ ό μεθα

   2. ἐ λύ ου   2. ἐ λύ ε σθε

   3. ἐ λύ ε το   3. ἐ λύ ο ντο

1. Note the structure of these forms. Since this is the middle and passive of a secondary tense, augment and the secondary endings are used.
2. Note also the presence of connecting vowels.

AORIST

Active

S. 1. ἔ λυ σα   P. 1. ἐ λύ σα μεν

   2. ἔ λυ σα ς   2. ἐ λύ σα τε

   3. ἔ λυ σε   3. ἔ λυ σα ν

1. The augment is prefixed to the verb stem since this is a secondary tense. This is also true of the middle and passive forms below.
2. The σα is the sign of the aorist.

Middle

S. 1. ἐ λυ σά μην   P. 1. ἐ λυ σά μεθα

   2. ἐ λύ σω   2. ἐ λύ σα σθε

   3. ἐ λύ σα το   3. ἐ λύ σα ντο

1. Note the structure of these forms. Since this is the middle of a secondary tense, augment and the secondary endings are used.
2. Note the absence of connecting vowels.

Passive

S. 1. ἐ λύ θη ν   P. 1. ἐ λύ θη μεν

   2. ἐ λύ θη ς   2. ἐ λύ θη τε

   3. ἐ λύ θη   3. ἐ λύ θη σα ν

1. Note the presence of augment.
2. Note also the θη combination which is the sign of the passive.

PERFECT

Active

S. 1. λέ λυ κ α   P. 1. λε λύ κ αμεν

2. λέ λυ κ ας   2. λε λύ κ ατε

3. λέ λυ κ ε   3. λε λύ κ ασι

1. The reduplication (λε pre-fixed to the verb stem) and the κ are characteristic of the perfect.

2. Note the similarity of the endings to those of the aor-ist.

Middle and Passive

S. 1. λέ λυ μαι   P. 1. λε λύ μεθα

2. λέ λυ σαι   2. λέ λυ σθε

3. λέ λυ ται   3. λέ λυ νται

1. Note the simplicity of the formation of this conjuga-tion. The reduplication (λε) is prefixed to the verb stem and the primary endings in their basic forms are added following the stem.

2. Note also the *absence* of κ (sign of the perfect) and the connecting vowels.

PLUPERFECT

Active

S. 1. ἐ λε λύ κ ειν   P. 1. ἐ λε λύ κ εμεν

2. ἐ λε λύ κ εις   2. ἐ λε λύ κ ειτε

3. ἐ λε λύ κ ει   3. ἐ λε λύ κ εισαν

In addition to the reduplication and the κ which are characteris-tics of the perfect tenses, the pluperfect also takes an augment since it is a secondary tense.

Middle and Passive

S. 1. ἐ λε λύ μην   P. 1. ἐ λε λύ μεθα

2. ἐ λέ λυ σο   2. ἐ λέ λυ σθε

3. ἐ λέ λυ το   3. ἐ λέ λυ ντο

1. As in the perfect middle and passive these forms are sim-ple and basic. The endings in their basic forms are added to the verb stem without a connecting vowel. There is reduplication and augment.

2. Note the *absence* of the κ (sign of the perfect.)

3. The pluperfect, both active and middle/passive, is ex-tremely rare in the New Testament.

31

The Verb "to be" in the Indicative Mood

PRESENT		IMPERFECT		FUTURE	
S. 1.	εἰμί	S. 1.	ἤμην	S. 1.	ἔσομαι
2.	εἶ	2.	ἦς	2.	ἔσῃ
3.	ἐστί(ν)	3.	ἦν	3.	ἔσται
P. 1.	ἐσμέν	P. 1.	ἦμεν	P. 1.	ἐσόμεθα
2.	ἐστέ	2.	ἦτε	2.	ἔσεσθε
3.	εἰσί(ν)	3.	ἦσαν	3.	ἔσονται

2. THE SUBJUNCTIVE MOOD

In the subjunctive mood only the present and aorist tenses are used. The distinction between the present tense and the aorist tense in the subjunctive mood is not one of time but of action. The present indicates continuing or repeated action while the aorist refers to punctiliar action.

PRESENT

Active

S. 1. λύ ω
   2. λύ ῃς
   3. λύ ῃ
P. 1. λύ ωμεν
   2. λύ ητε
   3. λύ ωσι

Note the similarity between these forms and those of the present indicative active. In the singular the endings have been lengthened. In the plural the connecting vowels have been lengthened.

Middle and Passive

S. 1. λύ ω μαι
   2. λύ ῃ
   3. λύ η ται
P. 1. λυ ώ μεθα
   2. λύ η σθε
   3. λύ ω νται

These forms are identical with those of the present indicative middle and passive except for the lengthened connecting vowels.

32

AORIST

Active

S. 1. λύ σ ω

2. λύ σ ῃς

3. λύ σ ῃ

P. 1. λύ σ ωμεν

2. λύ σ ητε

3. λύ σ ωσι

The aorist is formed by inserting a σ following the verb stem. Note the same phenomenon in the aorist subjunctive middle. This is what would be expected in the future subjunctive active if there were such a conjugation.

Middle

S. 1. λύ σ ω μαι   P. 1. λυ σ ώ μεθα

2. λύ σ ῃ   2. λύ σ η σθε

3. λύ σ η ται   3. λύ σ ω νται

Passive

S. 1. λυ θ ῶ

2. λυ θ ῇς

3. λυ θ ῇ

P. 1. λυ θ ῶμεν

2. λυ θ ῆτε

3. λυ θ ῶσι

1. Note the presence of the θη combination which is the sign of the passive voice.

2. Note also that the endings are identical to those of the present and aorist tenses. The accent is a circumflex throughout.

Present Subjunctive of the Verb "to be"

S. 1. ὦ

2. ῇς

3. ῇ

P. 1. ὦμεν

2. ἦτε

3. ὦσι

1. These forms correspond exactly to the endings of the aorist subjunctive passive.

2. Note the smooth breathing and the circumflex accent throughout.

33

Uses of the Subjunctive

1. In the protasis of future more vivid and present general conditional sentences (ἐάν plus the subjunctive).

2. To express an exhortation. This is called a hortatory subjunctive.

3. In final (also called purpose or telic) clauses. Such clauses are introduced by the words ἵνα, ὡς, or ὅπως.

4. After verbs of fearing with the negative particle μή.

5. The aorist subjunctive is used with the negative particle μή to express prohibitions (of acts not yet begun).

6. In deliberative questions (that is, a question which implies an answer in the imperative mood).

---

3. THE IMPERATIVE MOOD

This mood is found primarily in the present and aorist tenses.
This mood has no first person, either singular or plural.

PRESENT

		Active				*Middle and Passive*
S.	2.	λῦ ε		S.	2.	λύ ου
	3.	λυ έ τω			3.	λυ έ σθω
P.	2.	λύ ε τε		P.	2.	λύ ε σθε
	3.	λυ έ τωσαν			3.	λυ έ σθωσαν
		or				or
		λυ ό ντων				λυ έ σθων

AORIST
Active

S.	2.	λῦ σ ον	P.	2.	λύ σα τε	
	3.	λυ σά τω		3.	λυ σά τωσαν or λυ σά ντων	

Middle

S.	2.	λῦ σα ι	
	3.	λυ σά σθω	
P.	2.	λύ σα σθε	
	3.	λυ σά σθωσαν	
		or	
		λυ σά σθων	

1. The aorist, though a secondary tense, has no augment in the imperative mood.

2. Note the presence of the characteristic sign of the aorist (σα) in the active and middle voices (except active second singular).

Passive

S.	2.	λύ θη τι	
	3.	λυ θή τω	
P.	2.	λύ θη τε	
	3.	λυ θή τωσαν	
		or	
		λυ θέ ντων	

Note the presence of the characteristic sign of the passive (θη) throughout except in the alternate form of the third person plural.

Present Imperative of the Verb "to be"

S.	2.	ἴσθι	P.	2.	ἔστε
	3.	ἔστω*		3.	ἔστωσαν or ἔστων

* The alternate form ἤτω also occurs. Cf. 1 Corinthians 16:22; James 5:12.

The Time Element in the Imperative

1. There is no distinction as to time between the present and the aorist tenses in the imperative mood.

2. The present imperative implies that the action expressed in the verb is continued or repeated.

3. The aorist imperative implies that the action expressed in the verb is not continued or repeated.

Uses of the Imperative

1. It may express an exhortation, entreaty, or command.

2. It expresses prohibition (of an act already begun) when used with the negative particle μή.

4. SPECIAL PROBLEMS

Verb Stems Ending in Mutes

$$\text{There are three kinds of mutes} \left.\begin{cases} \text{Labial} - \pi, \beta, \phi \\ \text{Palatal} - \kappa, \gamma, \chi \\ \text{Dental} - \tau, \delta, \theta \end{cases}\right.$$

In the future and aorist tenses where these mutes meet the σ characteristic of these tenses, contractions take place which are illustrated in the following chart.

$$\pi, \beta, \phi + \sigma = \psi$$
$$\kappa, \gamma, \chi + \sigma = \xi$$
$$\tau, \delta, \theta + \sigma = \sigma$$

In the perfect and pluperfect tenses where these mutes meet the κ characteristic of these tenses, contractions take place which are illustrated in the following chart.

$$\pi, \beta, \phi + \kappa = \phi$$
$$\kappa, \gamma, \chi + \kappa = \chi$$
$$\tau, \delta, \theta + \kappa = \kappa$$

In the forms of the passive voice where these mutes meet the θ characteristic of the passive, contractions take place which are illustrated in the following chart.

$$\pi, \beta, \phi + \theta = \phi\theta$$
$$\kappa, \gamma, \chi + \theta = \chi\theta$$
$$\tau, \delta, \theta + \theta = \sigma\theta$$

Reduplication in the Perfect and Pluperfect Tenses

Reduplication is usually accomplished by:

1. Repeating the initial letter of verbs beginning with a consonant and prefixing this letter, followed by an ϵ, to the verb stem.

2. Lengthening the initial vowel of verbs whose stems begin with a vowel according to the rules of temporal augment.

When a verb stem begins with a rough mute (ϕ, χ, θ) the cognate smooth form of the mute (π, κ, τ) is used with the ϵ to accomplish reduplication.

When a verb stem begins with more than one consonant, or with one of the double consonants (ξ, ζ, ψ, ρ), reduplication is accomplished by means of a syllabic augment.

Stems With Final Vowels in the Future, Aorist and Perfect Tenses

When the verb stem ends with a vowel, that vowel is regularly lengthened before the σ of the future and aorist tenses and before the κ of the perfect and pluperfect tenses.

5. CONTRACT VERBS

General Observations and Rules

1. Contract verbs are verbs whose stems end with one of the short vowels, a, ϵ, or o.
2. They are called "contract" verbs because of the contraction which takes place when the short final vowel of the stem comes into contact with the vowels or diphthongs of the personal endings.
3. Due to the nature of the personal endings in the various tenses *the contractions take place only in the present and the imperfect tenses* of the finite verb. Contraction is found in all forms of the declension of the participles.
4. Those forms affected by the contractions include all voices of the present and imperfect tenses in the indicative, subjunctive, imperative, and optative moods.
5. The lexicon or vocabulary list will give the verb in its uncontracted form.
6. In those situations where the final short vowel of the verb stem is joined to a tense suffix which does not begin with a vowel or diphthong (future, aorist, etc.) the final short vowel is lengthened to its corresponding long vowel.

Examples

τιμάω (τιμῶ, contracted form) becomes τιμήσω in the future.

ποιέω (ποιῶ, contracted form) becomes ποιήσω in the future.

πληρόω (πληρῶ, contracted form) becomes πληρώσω in the future.

Accenting Contract Verbs

1. The accent is recessive in the *uncontracted form.*
2. If either of the two uncontracted syllables has the accent, the contracted syllable will also be accented.
3. If the contracted syllable is to be accented and is the ultima it will take a circumflex accent.
4. Elsewhere the general rules of accenting apply.
   Example – τιμάω becomes τιμῶ.

Rules for Contractions

EXAMPLES

α Type τιμάω – "honor"

α + ω, ο, or ου = ω	τιμά	+ ω	= τιμῶ
	τιμά	+ ομεν	= τιμῶμεν
	τιμά	+ ουσι	= τιμῶσι

| α + ει or ῃ = ᾳ | τιμά | + ει | = τιμᾷ |
| | τιμά | + ῃ | = τιμᾷ |

| α + ε or η = long α | τιμά | + ετε | = τιμᾶτε |
| | τιμά | + ητε | = τιμᾶτε |

ε Type ποιέω – "do, make"

| ε + ω = ω | ποιέ | + ω | = ποιῶ |

| ε + ο or ου = ου | ποιέ | + ομεν | = ποιοῦμεν |
| | ποιέ | + ουσι | = ποιοῦσι |

| ε + ε or ει = ει | ποιέ | + ετε | = ποιεῖτε |
| | ποιέ | + ει | = ποιεῖ |

| ε + η = η | ποιέ | + ητε | = ποιῆτε |

| ε + ῃ = ῃ | ποιέ | + ῃ | = ποιῇ |

ο Type πληρόω – "fill"

| ο + ω or η = ω | πληρό | + ω | = πληρῶ |
| | πληρό | + ητε | = πληρῶτε |

ο + ο, ε, or ου = ου	πληρό	+ ομεν	= πληροῦμεν
	πληρό	+ ετε	= πληροῦτε
	πληρό	+ ουσι	= πληροῦσι

| ο + ει or ῃ = οι | πληρό | + ει | = πληροῖ |
| | πληρό | + ης | = πληροῖς |

Exceptions to Rules for Contractions

1. The present active infinitive of the a type is contracted from $a + \epsilon \nu$ to $\bar{a}\nu$ rather than $\dot{\bar{a}}\nu$.

2. The present active infinitive of the o type is contracted from $o + \epsilon \nu$ to $o\bar{\upsilon}\nu$ rather than $o\bar{\iota}\nu$.

6. LIQUID VERBS

General Observations and Rules

1. A liquid verb is a verb whose stem ends in one of the so-called liquid consonants, λ, μ, ν, or ρ.

2. The peculiarities in the liquid verbs are limited to the future and first aorist tenses. The reason for this is that the liquid consonant rejects the σ which is characteristically present in both of these tenses.

3. Compensation for this rejection takes place in two ways.

    a. In the future an ϵ is added to the stem. The verb is then treated like a contract verb of the ϵ type.

    Example — The future of $\mu \acute{\epsilon}\nu\omega$ should logically be $\mu \acute{\epsilon}\nu\sigma\omega$. The σ, however, is dropped and an ϵ is inserted resulting in the form, $\mu \epsilon\nu \acute{\epsilon}\omega$. This is then contracted to $\mu \epsilon\nu \hat{\omega}$.

    b. In the aorist the short vowel preceding the liquid is lengthened according to the following pattern:

a	becomes	η
ϵ	becomes	$\epsilon\iota$
short ι	becomes	long ι

    Example — According to the rules for constructing the aorist we would assume the aorist form of $\mu \acute{\epsilon}\nu\omega$ to be $\check{\epsilon}\mu \epsilon\nu\sigma\alpha$. The liquid rejects the σ leaving the form $\check{\epsilon}\mu \epsilon\nu\alpha$. The ϵ preceding the liquid is lengthened to $\epsilon\iota$ resulting in the form, $\check{\epsilon}\mu \epsilon\iota\nu\alpha$.

4. In the subjunctive mood the peculiarities connected with the liquid verbs are found only in the aorist since there is no future subjunctive.

5. These peculiarities also affect the imperative mood of the finite verb, the infinitive, and the participles.

39

REPRESENTATIVE CONJUGATIONS

μένω – "remain"

Future Indicative Middle

S. 1. μεν οῦ μαι   P. 1. μεν οὐ μεθα

2. μεν ῇ   2. μεν εῖ σθε

3. μεν εῖ ται   3. μεν οῦ νται

Aorist Indicative Active

S. 1. ἔ μειν α   P. 1. ἐ μείν αμεν

2. ἔ μειν ας   2. ἐ μείν ατε

3. ἔ μειν ε   3. ἔ μειν αν

Aorist Subjunctive Middle

S. 1. μείν ω μαι   P. 1. μειν ώ μεθα

2. μείν ῃ   2. μείν η σθε

3. μείν η ται   3. μείν ω νται

C. THE MI CONJUGATION

1. INTRODUCTION

Due to the numerous irregularities that occur in the μι verbs, it is especially important for the student to become familiar with those features which the various verbs of this conjugation have in common. It is also important that the irregularities be noted. This may be done only by continual reference to a lexicon or New Testament Greek grammar.

Since δίδωμι is one of the most regular of the μι verbs it will be used to illustrate the construction of the verbs of this conjugation. The same procedure will be followed as with the verbs of the ω conjugation (i.e., the forms will be charted according to mood).

The forms of other μι verbs should be learned by comparison and contrast with δίδωμι.

It is very important that the principle parts of the μι verbs be memorized, since it is virtually impossible to construct or identify the various forms without this knowledge.

Characteristics of the μι Verbs

1. These verbs are so named because the first person singular, present indicative active ends in μι rather than ω.

2. The stem of the verb is often not recognizable and must be learned from a lexicon.

3. μι verbs *do not* have connecting vowels in the present, imperfect, and aorist tenses.

4. μι verbs have reduplication in the present and imperfect tenses as well as in the perfect and the pluperfect tenses. This reduplication is formed by repeating the initial consonant (when this is a rough mute its cognate smooth form is used) with an ι rather than an ε.

5. In the singular of the present and imperfect tenses the stem vowel is lengthened.

6. Verbs of the μι conjugation differ radically from verbs of the ω conjugation only in the present and *second* aorist systems.

41

2. THE INDICATIVE MOOD

$\delta\iota\delta\omega\mu\iota$ – "give"

PRESENT

Active

S. 1. $\delta\iota\ \delta\omega\ \mu\iota$ P. 1. $\delta\iota\ \delta o\ \mu\epsilon\nu$

2. $\delta\iota\ \delta\omega\ \varsigma$ 2. $\delta\iota\ \delta o\ \tau\epsilon$

3. $\delta\iota\ \delta\omega\ \sigma\iota$ 3. $\delta\iota\ \delta\acute{o}\ \alpha\sigma\iota$

1. The endings must be committed to memory. However, note the similarities between the plural endings and the plural endings of the present indicative active of the ω conjugation.

2. Note that in the singular the o of the stem is lengthened to an ω.

Middle and Passive

S. 1. $\delta\iota\ \delta o\ \mu\alpha\iota$ P. 1. $\delta\iota\ \delta\acute{o}\ \mu\epsilon\theta\alpha$

2. $\delta\iota\ \delta o\ \sigma\alpha\iota$ 2. $\delta\iota\ \delta o\ \sigma\theta\epsilon$

3. $\delta\iota\ \delta o\ \tau\alpha\iota$ 3. $\delta\iota\ \delta o\ \nu\tau\alpha\iota$

1. This conjugation is formed by adding the basic primary endings to the verb stem.

2. The characteristic reduplication should also be noted.

FUTURE

Active

S. 1. $\delta\acute{\omega}\ \sigma\ \omega$ P. 1. $\delta\acute{\omega}\ \sigma\ o\ \mu\epsilon\nu$

2. $\delta\acute{\omega}\ \sigma\ \epsilon\iota\varsigma$ 2. $\delta\acute{\omega}\ \sigma\ \epsilon\ \tau\epsilon$

3. $\delta\acute{\omega}\ \sigma\ \epsilon\iota$ 3. $\delta\acute{\omega}\ \sigma\ o\upsilon\ \sigma\iota$

1. The o of the verb stem is lengthened to an ω according to the rule that if the verb stem ends with a vowel that vowel is lengthened before the σ of the future.

2. σ, the sign of the future, follows the stem.

3. The endings conform exactly to those of the future indicative active of the ω conjugation.

Middle

S. 1. $\delta\acute{\omega}\ \sigma\ o\ \mu\alpha\iota$ P. 1. $\delta\omega\ \sigma\ \acute{o}\ \mu\epsilon\theta\alpha$

2. $\delta\acute{\omega}\ \sigma\ \eta$ 2. $\delta\acute{\omega}\ \sigma\ \epsilon\ \sigma\theta\epsilon$

3. $\delta\acute{\omega}\ \sigma\ \epsilon\ \tau\alpha\iota$ 3. $\delta\acute{\omega}\ \sigma\ o\ \nu\tau\alpha\iota$

1. For the same reason as in the future active above, the o of the verb stem is lengthened to an ω.

2. σ, the sign of the future, follows the stem.

3. The connecting vowels (o before μ and ν; ϵ elsewhere) follow the σ.

4. The primary endings are then added.

Passive

S. 1. δω θή σ ο μαι

2. δω θή σ ῃ

3. δω θή σ ε ται

P. 1. δω θη σ ό μεθα

2. δω θή σ ε σθε

3. δω θή σ ο νται

To the stem δω (*o* lengthened to ω) are added in the following order:

1. θη, the sign of the passive.
2. σ, the sign of the future.
3. The proper connecting vowel.
4. The primary endings.

IMPERFECT

Active

S. 1. ἐ δί δο υν

2. ἐ δί δο υς

3. ἐ δί δο υ

P. 1. ἐ δί δο μεν

2. ἐ δί δο τε

3. ἐ δί δο σαν

1. This conjugation bears a marked resemblance to the imperfect indicative active in the ω conjugation.
2. Note the endings and the augment. There is, of course, the reduplication characteristic of the imperfect of the μι verbs.

Middle and Passive

S. 1. ἐ δι δό μην

2. ἐ δί δο σο

3. ἐ δί δο το

P. 1. ἐ δι δό μεθα

2. ἐ δί δο σθε

3. ἐ δί δο ντο

1. This conjugation is formed by adding the basic secondary endings to the verb stem.
2. The reduplication characteristic of the imperfect of the μι verbs and the augment characteristic of verbs of the secondary tenses in the indicative mood should also be noted.

SECOND AORIST

Active

S. 1. ἔ δω κ α

2. ἔ δω κ ας

3. ἔ δω κ ε

P. 1. ἐ δώ κ αμεν

2. ἐ δώ κ ατε

3. ἔ δω κ αν

a. The endings are exactly the same, except that κ has replaced σ, for this is, in reality, a first aorist form. It is used since the second aorist indicative active does not occur in this verb.

b. The augment characteristic of secondary tenses in the indicative mood is present.

1. Note the similarities between these and the first aorist indicative active forms of the ω conjugation.

2. Also note that the o of the stem is lengthened to an ω (see note 2 under perfect active, p. 45, relating to this).

Middle

S. 1. ἐ δό μην

2. ἔ δο υ

3. ἔ δο το

P. 1. ἐ δό μεθα

2. ἔ δο σθε

3. ἔ δο ντο

Since this is a *second* aorist this conjugation bears marked similarities to the imperfect tense.

1. There is augment.

2. The basic secondary endings are used (except in the second person singular where a contraction takes place).

Passive

S. 1. ἐ δό θη ν

2. ἐ δό θη ς

3. ἐ δό θη

P. 1. ἐ δό θη μεν

2. ἐ δό θη τε

3. ἐ δό θη σαν

ative passive of the ω conjugation.

1. An augment is prefixed to the stem.

2. The θη combination (sign of the passive) follows the stem.

3. The first aorist indicative passive endings of the ω conjugation are then added.

These forms follow exactly the forms of the first aorist indic-

PERFECT

Active

	S.				P.		
	1.	δέ δω κ α			1.	δε δώ κ αμεν	
	2.	δέ δω κ ας			2.	δε δώ κ ατε	
	3.	δέ δω κ ε			3.	δε δώ κ ασι	
						or	
						δέ δω κ αν	

1. This paradigm is perfectly regular in that it follows exactly that of the perfect indicative active in the ω conjugation. Note the reduplication, the presence of the κ, and the endings.

2. The o is lengthened to an ω according to the rule that if the verb stem ends with a vowel that vowel is lengthened before the κ of the perfect.

Middle and Passive

	S.				P.		
	1.	δέ δο μαι			1.	δε δό μεθα	
	2.	δέ δο σαι			2.	δέ δο σθε	
	3.	δέ δο ται			3.	δέ δο νται	

This paradigm follows exactly that of the perfect indicative middle and passive of the ω conjugation.

PLUPERFECT

Active

	S.				P.		
	1.	ἐ δε δώ κ εⲱ			1.	ἐ δε δώ κ εμεν	
	2.	ἐ δε δώ κ εις			2.	ἐ δε δώ κ ειτε	
	3.	ἐ δε δώ κ ει			3.	ἐ δε δώ κ εισαν	

1. The same facts noted in connection with the perfect active are applicable to the pluperfect active.
2. Note also the augment which is present because the pluperfect is a secondary tense.
3. This tense is very rare in the New Testament.

Middle and Passive

	S.				P.		
	1.	ἐ δε δό μην			1.	ἐ δε δό μεθα	
	2.	ἐ δέ δο σο			2.	ἐ δέ δο σθε	
	3.	ἐ δέ δο το			3.	ἐ δέ δο ντο	

This paradigm follows exactly that of the pluperfect indicative middle and passive of the ω conjugation.

3. THE SUBJUNCTIVE MOOD

It should be remembered that *only* the present and aorist tenses appear in the subjunctive mood.

The subjunctive of the $\mu\iota$ verbs should be studied by comparing and contrasting the various conjugations with the corresponding paradigms in the ω conjugation.

PRESENT

	S.	1. δι δῶ		P.	1. δι δῶ μεν
Active		2. δι δῷ ς			2. δι δῶ τε
		3. δι δῷ			3. δι δῶ σι

1. Note the reduplication characteristic of the $\mu\iota$ verbs.
2. The endings are formed by contracting the *o* of the verb stem with the initial vowels of the endings of the present active subjunctive of the ω conjugation.

Note that $o + \eta = \omega$, not $o\iota$ as in ω conjugation verbs.

	S.	1. δι δῶ μαι		P.	1. δι δῶ μεθα
Middle and Passive		2. δι δῷ			2. δι δῶ σθε
		3. δι δῶ ται			3. δι δῶ νται

1. The same facts noted in connection with the present active subjunctive should also be noted here.
2. The basic primary endings are used except in the second person singular, where several contractions take place.

SECOND AORIST

Active				*Middle*			
S.	1. δῶ	P.	1. δῶ μεν	S.	1. δῶ μαι	P.	1. δῶ μεθα
	2. δῷ ς		2. δῶ τε		2. δῷ		2. δῶ σθε
	3. δῷ		3. δῶ σι		3. δῶ ται		3. δῶ νται

These forms are identical to those of the present subjunctive except that there is no reduplication.

46

4. THE IMPERATIVE MOOD

It should be remembered that this mood is found primarily in the present and the aorist tenses.

PRESENT

Active

S. 2. δί δο υ   P. 2. δί δο τε

    3. δι δό τω   3. δι δό τωσαν or δι δό ντων

Note the following:

1. The reduplication characteristic of the μι verbs.

2. The use of the basic stem (δο) in all forms except the second person singular, where a contraction has taken place.

3. The endings are exactly the same as those of the corresponding paradigm in the ω conjugation.

Middle and Passive

S. 2. δί δο σο   P. 2. δί δο σθε

    3. δι δό σθω   3. δι δό σθωσαν or δι δό σθων

The same facts noted in connection with the present active imperative should also be noted here.

AORIST

Active

S. 2. δό ς   P. 2. δό τε

    3. δό τω   3. δό τωσαν or δό ντων

These forms are basically the same as those of the present imperative except for,

1. The absence of the reduplication.
2. The second person singular ending.

Middle

S. 2. δο ῦ   P. 2. δό σθε

    3. δό σθω   3. δό σθωσαν or δό σθων

These forms are basically the same as those of the present except for,

1. The absence of reduplication.
2. The second person singular ending.

5. MI VERBS USED IN THE NEW TESTAMENT

Only the basic forms of the verbs used in the New Testament are given. Many also are found in composition (i.e., with preposition prefixed). These are not given unless only forms in composition appear in the New Testament.

The stems of the verbs are given in the parentheses following the verbs.

*† ἀμφιέννυμι (ἐ) – "clothe, dress"

*† ἀπόλλυμι (ολ) – "ruin, destroy"

† δείκνυμι (δεικ) – "show"

δίδωμι (δο) – "give"

‡ δύναμαι (δυνα) – "can, be able"

† εἰμί (εσ) – "be, exist"

† εἶμι (ι)[1] – "go"

*† ἐκπετάννυμι (πετα) – "spread"

*† ἐπίσταμαι (στα) – "understand, know"

† ζώννυμι (ζω) – "gird"

* ἵημι (ἐ) – "send"

ἵστημι (στα) – "put, place"

*† κάθημαι (ἡς) – "sit"

*† κατάγνυμι (αγ) – "break"

‡ κεῖμαι (κει) – "lie, recline"

† κεράννυμι (κερα) – "mix"

κίχρημι (χρα) – "lend"

† κορέννυμι (κορε) – "satiate, fill"

‡† κρέμαμαι (κρεμα) – "hang, suspend"

† κρεμάννυμι (κρεμα) – "hang, suspend"

† μίγνυμι[2] (μιγ) – "mix, mingle"

† ὄμνυμι[3] (ομ) – "swear, take an oath"

ὀνίνημι (ονα) – "be useful, help"[4]

† πήγνυμι (παγ) – "fix, build"

πίμπλημι (πλα) – "fill"

πίμπρημι (πρα) – "burn with fever, swell up"

† ῥήγνυμι (ῥαγ) – "tear, break"

† ῥώννυμι (ῥω) – "strengthen, make strong"

† σβέννυμι (σβε) – "extinguish, put out"

† στρώννυμι[5] (στρω) – "spread"

τίθημι (θε) – "put, place"

† φημί (φα) – "say, affirm"

---

* appears only in composition   ‡ deponent   † without reduplication

1. Whether or not this verb appears in the New Testament is debated by scholars. Some accept it as the correct reading in John 7:34, 36. There is no question, however, that it does appear in composition with ἀπ–, εἴ–, εἴς–, ἔξ–, ἔπ–, and σύν–.
2. Also appears in the New Testament under the forms μείγνυμι and μειγνύω.
3. The by-form ὀμνύω also appears in the New Testament.
4. In the New Testament this verb is found only in the middle voice with the meaning "may I have joy."
5. Also appears in the New Testament under the form στρωννύω.

D. IRREGULAR VERBS

A common phenomenon of language is what is known as the "irregular" verb. An irregular verb is exactly as the name implies, a verb that is irregular in the formation of its principal parts.

A verb such as λύω is considered a "regular" verb since the basic verb stem is evident in all the principal parts and since it follows all the regular rules for the construction of a verb as noted elsewhere. An irregular verb, however, may vary quite radically from form to form. The basic verb stem may not be in evidence at all in some forms of the irregular verbs. In fact, in the principal parts of some irregular verbs two or even three different verb stems may be in evidence.

The only way to assure immediate recognition of any given form of an irregular verb is by committing these forms to memory. Since the New Testament contains a multitude of irregular verbs, some of which appear in only one or, at most, several forms, no attempt has been made to include all. Listed below are the principal parts of 37 major irregular verbs which appear in the New Testament. These particular verbs have been chosen for any or all of three possible reasons:

1. They are used quite often in the New Testament.

2. They appear in the New Testament quite regularly in composition with various prepositions.

3. Their principal parts may give certain clues as to the formation of the principal parts of other verbs.

The principal parts of a verb are the first person singular indicative of the following tenses: present active, future active, aorist active, perfect active, perfect middle/passive, and aorist passive.

By careful examination of the forms below it may be noted that some of the forms are not as irregular as they may appear to be at first glance. Consider, for example, the future form of ἄγω which is ἄξω. In the section entitled "Construction of Verbs" it was pointed out that σ is the sign of the future. Under "Special Problems" it was noted that when a verb stem ending with a γ is followed by the σ of the future, the γσ is contracted to ξ. Thus ἄγ + σω = ἄξω.

49

PRINCIPAL PARTS OF IRREGULAR VERBS

Present Active	Future Active	Aorist Active	Perfect Active	Perfect Mid./Pass.	Aorist Passive	English Meaning
ἀγγέλλω	ἀγγελῶ	ἤγγειλα		ἤγγελμαι	ἠγγέλην	announce
ἄγω	ἄξω	ἤγαγον	ἦχα*	ἦγμαι	ἤχθην	lead
αἴρω	ἀρῶ	ἦρα	ἦρκα	ἦρμαι	ἤρθην	lift up
αἱρέω	ἑλῶ	εἷλον	ᾕρηκα	ᾕρημαι	ᾑρέθην	take
ἀκούω	ἀκούσω[1]	ἤκουσα	ἀκήκοα	ἤκουσμαι*	ἠκούσθην	hear
ἁμαρτάνω	ἁμαρτήσω[2]	ἡμάρτησα or ἥμαρτον[3]	ἡμάρτηκα	ἡμάρτημαι*	ἡμαρτήθην	sin
ἀπόλλυμι	ἀπολέσω	ἀπώλεσα	ἀπώλωλα			destroy
βαίνω[4]	βήσομαι	ἔβην	βέβηκα	βέβαμαι*	ἐβάθην*	go
βάλλω	βαλῶ	ἔβαλον	βέβληκα	βέβλημαι	ἐβλήθην	throw
βούλομαι[5]	βουλήσομαι*	ἐβουλόμην		βεβούλημαι*	ἐβουλήθην	desire
γίνομαι[6]	γενήσομαι	ἐγενόμην	γέγονα	γεγένημαι	ἐγενήθην	become
γινώσκω[7]	γνώσομαι	ἔγνων	ἔγνωκα	ἔγνωσμαι	ἐγνώσθην	know
γράφω	γράψω	ἔγραψα	γέγραφα	γέγραμμαι	ἐγράφην	write
διδάσκω	διδάξω	ἐδίδαξα	δεδίδαχα*	δεδίδαγμαι*	ἐδιδάχθην	teach
δίδωμι	δώσω	ἔδωκα	δέδωκα	δέδομαι	ἐδόθην	give
διώκω	διώξω	ἐδίωξα	δεδίωκα	δεδίωγμαι	ἐδιώχθην	run
δύναμαι	δυνήσομαι	ἐδυνάμην or ἠδυνάμην		δεδύνημαι*	ἠδυνήθην[8] or ἠδυνάσθην	can, be able

---

* Indicates that no form of this conjugation appears in the New Testament
1. This form represents a change from the Classical Greek form which was deponent (ἀκούσομαι).
2. In Classical Greek the form was ἁμαρτήσομαι.
3. In Classical Greek only ἥμαρτον appears.
4. This verb appears only in composition (i.e., in combination with a preposition) in the New Testament.
5. Note that in Luke 22:42 the form βούλει appears.
6. In Classical Greek the spelling is γίγνομαι .
7. In Classical Greek the spelling is γιγνώσκω.
8. In Classical Greek the spelling is ἐδυνήθην.

Present Active	Future Active	Aorist Active	Perfect Active	Perfect Mid./Pass.	Aorist Passive	English Meaning
ἐγείρω	ἐγερῶ	ἤγειρα	ἐγήγερκα	ἐγήγερμαι	ἠγέρθην	raise
ἔρχομαι	ἐλεύσομαι	ἦλθον	ἐλήλυθα			come
ἐσθίω	φάγομαι[9]	ἔφαγον				eat
εὑρίσκω	εὑρήσω	εὗρον	εὕρηκα	εὕρημαι*	εὑρέθην	find
ἔχω[10]	ἕξω	ἔσχον	ἔσχηκα	ἔσχημαι*		have
θνήσκω*	θανοῦμαι*	ἔθανον*	τέθνηκα			die
ἵστημι	στήσω	ἔστησα	ἕστηκα	ἔσταμαι*	ἐστάθην	stand
καλέω	καλέσω	ἐκάλεσα	κέκληκα	κέκλημαι	ἐκλήθην	call
κρίνω	κρινῶ	ἔκρινα	κέκρικα	κέκριμαι	ἐκρίθην	judge
λαμβάνω	λήμψομαι[11]	ἔλαβον	εἴληφα	εἴλημμαι	ἐλήμφθην[12]	take
μένω	μενῶ	ἔμεινα	μεμένηκα			remain
ὁράω	ὄψομαι	εἶδον	ἑώρακα or ἑόρακα	ὦμμαι*	ὤφθην	see
πάσχω	πείσομαι*	ἔπαθον	πέπονθα			suffer
πίπτω	πεσοῦμαι	ἔπεσον or ἔπεσα	πέπτωκα			fall
στρέφω	στρέψω	ἔστρεψα		ἔστραμμαι	ἐστράφην	turn
σώζω	σώσω	ἔσωσα	σέσωκα	σέσωμαι or σέσωσμαι*	ἐσώθην	save
τάσσω	τάξω	ἔταξα	τέταχα	τέταγμαι	ἐτάγην	arrange
τίθημι	θήσω	ἔθηκα	τέθεικα	τέθειμαι	ἐτέθην	place
φέρω	οἴσω	ἤνεγκα	ἐνήνοχα	ἐνήνεγμαι*	ἠνέχθην	bear
φημί[13]	ἐρῶ	εἶπον	εἴρηκα	εἴρημαι	ἐρρέθην or ἐρρήθην	say

9. In Classical Greek the form ἔδομαι appears.
10. In Classical Greek the form σχήσω also appears.
11. In Classical Greek the spelling is λήψομαι.
12. In Classical Greek the spelling is ἐλήφθην.
13. These principal parts may also be identified with the verb λέγω.

* Indicates that no form of this conjugation appears in the New Testament

IV. PRONOUNS

PRONOUNS

INTENSIVE

αὐτός — "himself"

		Masculine	Feminine	Neuter
S.	N.	αὐτός	αὐτή	αὐτό
	G.	αὐτοῦ	αὐτῆς	αὐτοῦ
	D.	αὐτῷ	αὐτῇ	αὐτῷ
	A.	αὐτόν	αὐτήν	αὐτό
P.	N.	αὐτοί	αὐταί	αὐτά
	G.	αὐτῶν	αὐτῶν	αὐτῶν
	D.	αὐτοῖς	αὐταῖς	αὐτοῖς
	A.	αὐτούς	αὐτάς	αὐτά

The declension of the intensive pronoun follows the declension of the vowel declension adjective ἀγαθός except in the nominative and accusative singular of the neuter.

The intensive pronoun is always used in apposition with a noun.

Uses of the Intensive Pronoun

1. As an intensive pronoun in all cases, i.e., "himself, herself, itself."

2. As a third person, personal pronoun in the oblique cases (i.e., all cases but the nominative).

3. To mean "the same" when used with the definite article.

DEMONSTRATIVE

οὗτος — "this"

		Masculine	Feminine	Neuter
S.	N.	οὗτος	αὕτη	τοῦτο
	G.	τούτου	ταὐτης	τούτου
	D.	τούτῳ	ταὐτῃ	τούτῳ
	A.	τοῦτον	ταὐτην	τοῦτο
P.	N.	οὗτοι	αὗται	ταῦτα
	G.	τούτων	τούτων	τούτων
	D.	τούτοις	ταὐταις	τούτοις
	A.	τούτους	ταὐτας	ταῦτα

Note the similarities between οὗτος and αὐτός.

The feminine genitive plural and the neuter nominative and accusative plurals should be noted for their peculiarities.

ἐκεῖνος — "that"

The declension of ἐκεῖνος follows that of αὐτός exactly.

When the demonstrative pronoun is used to modify a noun, the noun takes the definite article and the pronoun then stands either before or after the noun and article.

REFLEXIVE

ἐμαυτοῦ– "myself"

The reflexive pronoun has no nominative forms.

First Person

		Masculine	Feminine
S.	G.	ἐμαυτοῦ	ἐμαυτῆς
	D.	ἐμαυτῷ	ἐμαυτῇ
	A.	ἐμαυτόν	ἐμαυτήν
P.	G.	ἐαυτῶν	ἐαυτῶν
	D.	ἐαυτοῖς	ἐαυταῖς
	A.	ἐαυτούς	ἐαυτάς

Second Person

		Masculine	Feminine
S.	G.	σεαυτοῦ	σεαυτῆς
	D.	σεαυτῷ	σεαυτῇ
	A.	σεαυτόν	σεαυτήν
P.	G	ἐαυτῶν	ἐαυτῶν
	D.	ἐαυτοῖς	ἐαυταῖς
	A.	ἐαυτούς	ἐαυτάς

Third Person

		Masculine	Feminine	Neuter
S.	G.	ἐαυτοῦ	ἐαυτῆς	ἐαυτοῦ
	D.	ἐαυτῷ	ἐαυτῇ	ἐαυτῷ
	A.	ἐαυτόν	ἐαυτήν	ἐαυτό
P.	G.	ἐαυτῶν	ἐαυτῶν	ἐαυτῶν
	D.	ἐαυτοῖς	ἐαυταῖς	ἐαυτοῖς
	A.	ἐαυτούς	ἐαυτάς	ἐαυτά

INTERROGATIVE

τίς — "who, which, what"

		Masculine and Feminine	Neuter
S.	N.	τίς	τί
	G.	τίνος	τίνος
	D.	τίνι	τίνι
	A.	τίνα	τί
P.	N.	τίνες	τίνα
	G.	τίνων	τίνων
	D.	τίσι	τίσι
	A.	τίνας	τίνα

The endings are those of the consonant declension nouns.

The intensive has an acute accent on the first syllable in all forms.

INDEFINITE

τις — "anyone, anything, something"

		Masculine and Feminine	Neuter
S.	N.	τις	τι
	G.	τινός	τινός
	D.	τινί	τινί
	A.	τινά	τι
P.	N.	τινές	τινά
	G.	τινῶν	τινῶν
	D.	τισί	τισί
	A.	τινάς	τινά

Note that the forms are exactly the same as the interrogative, except for accent. All forms are accented on the ultima or not at all.

PERSONAL

		First Person ἐγώ – "I"	Second Person σύ – "you"	Third Person
S.	N.	ἐγώ	σύ	
	G.	ἐμοῦ (μου)	σοῦ	The third person does not have its own forms. The *Intensive* pronoun is used as a third person personal pronoun.
	D.	ἐμοί (μοι)	σοί	
	A.	ἐμέ (με)	σέ	
P.	N.	ἡμεῖς	ὑμεῖς	
	G.	ἡμῶν	ὑμῶν	
	D.	ἡμῖν	ὑμῖν	
	A.	ἡμᾶς	ὑμᾶς	

RELATIVE

ὅς — "who, which, what, that"

		Masculine	Feminine	Neuter
S.	N.	ὅς	ἥ	ὅ
	G.	οὗ	ἧς	οὗ
	D.	ᾧ	ᾗ	ᾧ
	A.	ὅν	ἥν	ὅ
P.	N.	οἵ	αἵ	ἅ
	G.	ὧν	ὧν	ὧν
	D.	οἷς	αἷς	οἷς
	A.	οὕς	ἅς	ἅ

The endings follow exactly those of the intensive pronoun. Note the rough breathings and the accents.

The relative pronoun will agree with its antecedent in gender and number but not necessarily in case. The case is determined by its use in its own clause.

RECIPROCAL

ἀλλήλων – "each other, one another"

This pronoun appears only in the genitive, dative, and accusative cases of the masculine plural.

The three forms are:

G. ἀλλήλων

D. ἀλλήλοις

A. ἀλλήλους

V. ADJECTIVES

ADJECTIVES

Vowel Declension Adjectives

ἀγαθός — "good"

		Masculine	*Feminine	Neuter
S.	N.	ἀγαθός	ἀγαθή	ἀγαθόν
	G.	ἀγαθοῦ	ἀγαθῆς	ἀγαθοῦ
	D.	ἀγαθῷ	ἀγαθῇ	ἀγαθῷ
	A.	ἀγαθόν	ἀγαθήν	ἀγαθόν
P.	N.	ἀγαθοί	ἀγαθαί	ἀγαθά
	G.	ἀγαθῶν	ἀγαθῶν	ἀγαθῶν
	D.	ἀγαθοῖς	ἀγαθαῖς	ἀγαθοῖς
	A.	ἀγαθούς	ἀγαθάς	ἀγαθά

μικρός — "small"

		Masculine	*Feminine	Neuter
S.	N.	μικρός	μικρά	μικρόν
	G.	μικροῦ	μικρᾶς	μικροῦ
	D.	μικρῷ	μικρᾷ	μικρῷ
	A.	μικρόν	μικράν	μικρόν
P.	N.	μικροί	μικραί	μικρά
	G.	μικρῶν	μικρῶν	μικρῶν
	D.	μικροῖς	μικραῖς	μικροῖς
	A.	μικρούς	μικράς	μικρά

*The difference in the endings is due to the application of the rule governing α declension nouns. Stems ending in ε, ι, or ρ take α endings. All others take η endings.

63

Consonant Declension Adjectives

πᾶς —"all, every"

		Masculine	Feminine	Neuter
S.	N.	πᾶς	πᾶσα	πᾶν
	G.	παντός	πάσης	παντός
	D.	παντί	πάσῃ	παντί
	A.	πάντα	πᾶσαν	πᾶν
P.	N.	πάντες	πᾶσαι	πάντα
	G.	πάντων	πασῶν	πάντων
	D.	πᾶσι	πάσαις	πᾶσι
	A.	πάντας	πάσας	πάντα

In this particular declension the masculine and neuter follow the consonant declension endings while the feminine follows the a declension short a type.

This illustrates the irregularities of the consonant declension adjectives, which are many. The student must learn these irregularities as they are encountered in translation.

A knowledge of the consonant declension nouns will help the student to learn the consonant declension adjectives.

Comparison of Adjectives

As in English, Greek adjectives have forms expressing relative differences in quality or quantity. In English the comparison is made as follows:

sweet, sweeter, sweetest

The basic form (sweet) is known as the positive, the second form (sweeter) is the comparative, while the final form (sweetest) is the superlative.

In Greek the positive form is that which is found in the lexicon as the most basic form (e.g., πιστός, "faithful").

Most adjectives form the comparative and superlative by adding τερος and τατος respectively to the stem. Thus the comparison of πιστός is,

πιστός, πιστότερος, πιστότατος

Some adjectives are compared by adding ιων and ιστος to the stem. For example,

$$κακός, \ κακίων, \ κάκιστος$$

Other adjectives are quite irregular in their comparison and must be memorized.

The comparative and superlative forms are declined in the same ways in which adjectives of the positive degree are declined.

VI. ADVERBS

ADVERBS

Most adverbs are formed by adding ως to the stem of the corresponding adjective. It may be convenient for the student to think of the adverb as being (empirically though not factually) formed on the basis of the genitive plural form of the adjective with the final ν being replaced by ς.

Consider the following examples:

Adjective	Genitive Plural	Adverb
δίκαιος – "just, righteous"	δικαίων	δικαίως – "justly"
κακός – "evil"	κακῶν	κακῶς – "badly"

The accent of the adverb generally remains the same as the accent of the genitive plural of the adjective. Note this in the examples above.

Adverbs, like adjectives, may be compared. The comparative degree of the adverb has the form of the neuter accusative singular of the comparative of the adjective, while the superlative degree has the form of the neuter accusative plural of the superlative of the adjective.

Consider the following examples:

Positive	Comparative	Superlative
δικαίως	δικαιότερον	δικαιότατα
καλῶς	κάλλιον	κάλλιστα

Note that, as with adjectives, many adverbs are quite irregular in their comparison and, therefore, must be committed to memory if they are to be easily recognized.

69

VII. PARTICIPLES

PARTICIPLES

A. BASIC GRAMMATICAL RULES

Time Element in Participles

1. Independently the participle has no reference to time.

2. The time element of the participle is always dependent on the time expressed in the finite verb.

   a. Action antecedent to the time of the finite verb is expressed by the aorist participle.

   b. Action contemporary to the time of the finite verb is expressed by the present participle.

   c. Action subsequent to the time of the finite verb is expressed by the future participle.

Use of Participles

The Greek participle is used:

1. Attributively — as an adjective.

2. Substantively — as a noun (usually with the definite article).

3. Circumstantially — as an adverb.

One of the circumstantial uses of the participle is the "genitive absolute." The participle will be in the genitive case with a noun in the genitive case, having no grammatical connection with the rest of the sentence.

B. PARTICIPLES OF Ω CONJUGATION VERBS

The present active participle and the present middle and passive participle should be learned as the basis for most of the other participial forms.

PRESENT ACTIVE PARTICIPLE

		Masculine	Feminine	Neuter
S.	N.	λύων	λύουσα	λῦον
	G.	λύοντος	λυούσης	λύοντος
	D.	λύοντι	λυούσῃ	λύοντι
	A.	λύοντα	λύουσαν	λῦον
P.	N.	λύοντες	λύουσαι	λύοντα
	G.	λυόντων	λυουσῶν	λυόντων
	D.	λύουσι	λυούσαις	λύουσι
	A.	λύοντας	λυούσας	λύοντα

1. The masculine and neuter forms take the consonant declension endings.
2. The feminine forms take the a declension endings.

PRESENT MIDDLE AND PASSIVE PARTICIPLE

		Masculine	Feminine	Neuter
S.	N.	λυόμενος	λυομένη	λυόμενον
	G.	λυομένου	λυομένης	λυομένου
	D.	λυομένῳ	λυομένῃ	λυομένῳ
	A.	λυόμενον	λυομένην	λυόμενον
P.	N.	λυόμενοι	λυόμεναι	λυόμενα
	G.	λυομένων	λυομένων	λυομένων
	D.	λυομένοις	λυομέναις	λυομένοις
	A.	λυομένους	λυομένας	λυόμενα

The endings are similar to those of the adjective.

FUTURE ACTIVE PARTICIPLE

		Masculine	Feminine	Neuter
S.	N.	λύσων	λύσουσα	λῦσον
	G.	λύσοντος	λυσούσης	λύσοντος
	D.	λύσοντι	λυσούσῃ	λύσοντι
	A.	λύσοντα	λύσουσαν	λῦσον
P.	N.	λύσοντες	λύσουσαι	λύσοντα
	G.	λυσόντων	λυσουσῶν	λυσόντων
	D.	λύσουσι	λυσούσαις	λύσουσι
	A.	λύσοντας	λυσούσας	λύσοντα

Note that the forms are the same as those of the present active participle except that σ, the sign of the future, is added to the verb stem.

FUTURE MIDDLE PARTICIPLE

		Masculine	Feminine	Neuter
S.	N.	λυσόμενος	λυσομένη	λυσόμενον
	G.	λυσομένου	λυσομένης	λυσομένου
	D.	λυσομένῳ	λυσομένῃ	λυσομένῳ
	A.	λυσόμενον	λυσομένην	λυσόμενον
P.	N.	λυσόμενοι	λυσόμεναι	λυσόμενα
	G.	λυσομένων	λυσομένων	λυσομένων
	D.	λυσομένοις	λυσομέναις	λυσομένοις
	A.	λυσομένους	λυσομένας	λυσόμενα

Note that the forms are the same as those of the present middle and passive participle except that σ, the sign of the future, follows the verb stem and precedes the connecting vowel and endings.

75

FUTURE PASSIVE PARTICIPLE

		Masculine	Feminine	Neuter
S.	N.	λυθησόμενος	λυθησομένη	λυθησόμενον
	G.	λυθησομένου	λυθησομένης	λυθησομένου
	D.	λυθησομένῳ	λυθησομένῃ	λυθησομένῳ
	A.	λυθησόμενον	λυθησομένην	λυθησόμενον
P.	N.	λυθησόμενοι	λυθησόμεναι	λυθησόμενα
	G.	λυθησομένων	λυθησομένων	λυθησομένων
	D.	λυθησομένοις	λυθησομέναις	λυθησομένοις
	A.	λυθησομένους	λυθησομένας	λυθησόμενα

Note that the same endings as those of the future middle participle are used with σ preceding the connecting vowels and endings but with θη, the sign of the passive, preceding the σ and following the verb stem.

AORIST ACTIVE PARTICIPLE

		Masculine	Feminine	Neuter
S.	N.	λύσας	λύσασα	λῦσαν
	G.	λύσαντος	λυσάσης	λύσαντος
	D.	λύσαντι	λυσάσῃ	λύσαντι
	A.	λύσαντα	λύσασαν	λῦσαν
P.	N.	λύσαντες	λύσασαι	λύσαντα
	G.	λυσάντων	λυσασῶν	λυσάντων
	D.	λύσασι	λυσάσαις	λύσασι
	A.	λύσαντας	λυσάσας	λύσαντα

1. Note the endings. In the masculine and neuter forms the consonant declension endings are used. The feminine forms are those of the α declension.

2. Note the presence of the σα, the sign of the aorist, which follows the verb stem and precedes the endings.

76

AORIST MIDDLE PARTICIPLE

		Masculine	Feminine	Neuter
S.	N.	λυσάμενος	λυσαμένη	λυσάμενον
	G.	λυσαμένου	λυσαμένης	λυσαμένου
	D.	λυσαμένῳ	λυσαμένῃ	λυσαμένῳ
	A.	λυσάμενον	λυσαμένην	λυσάμενον
P.	N.	λυσάμενοι	λυσάμεναι	λυσάμενα
	G.	λυσαμένων	λυσαμένων	λυσαμένων
	D.	λυσαμένοις	λυσαμέναις	λυσαμένοις
	A.	λυσαμένους	λυσαμένας	λυσάμενα

Note the following contrasts between the aorist middle participle and the present middle and passive participle:

1. The absence of the connecting vowel in the aorist middle participle.

2. The presence of σα, the sign of the aorist, in the aorist middle participle.

AORIST PASSIVE PARTICIPLE

		Masculine	Feminine	Neuter
S.	N.	λυθείς	λυθεῖσα	λυθέν
	G.	λυθέντος	λυθείσης	λυθέντος
	D.	λυθέντι	λυθείσῃ	λυθέντι
	A.	λυθέντα	λυθεῖσαν	λυθέν
P.	N.	λυθέντες	λυθεῖσαι	λυθέντα
	G.	λυθέντων	λυθεισῶν	λυθέντων
	D.	λυθεῖσι	λυθείσαις	λυθεῖσι
	A.	λυθέντας	λυθείσας	λυθέντα

1. Note the presence of θε, a variation of the sign of the passive.

2. The masculine and neuter endings are basically those of the consonant declension, liquid type. The feminine forms follow the a declension, short a type.

77

PERFECT ACTIVE PARTICIPLE

		Masculine	Feminine	Neuter
S.	N.	λελυκώς	λελυκυῖα	λελυκός
	G.	λελυκότος	λελυκυίας	λελυκότος
	D.	λελυκότι	λελυκυίᾳ	λελυκότι
	A.	λελυκότα	λελυκυῖαν	λελυκός
P.	N.	λελυκότες	λελυκυῖαι	λελυκότα
	G.	λελυκότων	λελυκυιῶν	λελυκότων
	D.	λελυκόσι	λελυκυίαις	λελυκόσι
	A.	λελυκότας	λελυκυίας	λελυκότα

1. Note the reduplication and the κ which are characteristic of the perfect tense.

2. The masculine and neuter endings are basically those of the consonant declension, mute type. The feminine forms follow the a declension, short a type.

PERFECT MIDDLE AND PASSIVE PARTICIPLE

		Masculine	Feminine	Neuter
S.	N.	λελυμένος	λελυμένη	λελυμένον
	G.	λελυμένου	λελυμένης	λελυμένου
	D.	λελυμένῳ	λελυμένῃ	λελυμένῳ
	A.	λελυμένον	λελυμένην	λελυμένον
P.	N.	λελυμένοι	λελυμέναι	λελυμένα
	G.	λελυμένων	λελυμένων	λελυμένων
	D.	λελυμένοις	λελυμέναις	λελυμένοις
	A.	λελυμένους	λελυμένας	λελυμένα

1. Note the reduplication characteristic of the perfect tense.

2. The endings are identical with those of the present middle and passive participle.

3. Note that the accent is on the penult throughout the declension.

PARTICIPLE OF THE VERB "TO BE"

		Masculine	Feminine	Neuter
S.	N.	ὤν	οὖσα	ὄν
	G.	ὄντος	οὔσης	ὄντος
	D.	ὄντι	οὔσῃ	ὄντι
	A.	ὄντα	οὖσαν	ὄν
P.	N.	ὄντες	οὖσαι	ὄντα
	G.	ὄντων	οὐσῶν	ὄντων
	D.	οὖσι	οὔσαις	οὖσι
	A.	ὄντας	οὔσας	ὄντα

1. The forms of the participle of the verb "to be" are identical to the endings of the present active participle.

2. The accent is on the initial syllable throughout except for the genitive plural in the feminine.

C. PARTICIPLES OF MI CONJUGATION VERBS

The participial forms of μι conjugation verbs should be learned, as far as possible, by comparison and contrast with the corresponding participial forms of ω conjugation verbs.

PRESENT ACTIVE PARTICIPLE

		Masculine	Feminine	Neuter
S.	N.	διδούς	διδοῦσα	διδόν
	G.	διδόντος	διδούσης	διδόντος
	D.	διδόντι	διδούσῃ	διδόντι
	A.	διδόντα	διδοῦσαν	διδόν
P.	N.	διδόντες	διδοῦσαι	διδόντα
	G.	διδόντων	διδουσῶν	διδόντων
	D.	διδοῦσι	διδούσαις	διδοῦσι
	A.	διδόντας	διδούσας	διδόντα

Note the following:

1. The reduplication characteristic of μι verbs in the present tense.
2. The masculine and neuter are declined using the third declension endings. The feminine is declined using the first declension endings.

PRESENT MIDDLE AND PASSIVE PARTICIPLE

		Masculine	Feminine	Neuter
S.	N.	διδόμενος	διδομένη	διδόμενον
	G.	διδομένου	διδομένης	διδομένου
	D.	διδομένῳ	διδομένῃ	διδομένῳ
	A.	διδόμενον	διδομένην	διδόμενον
P.	N.	διδόμενοι	διδόμεναι	διδόμενα
	G.	διδομένων	διδομενῶν	διδομένων
	D.	διδομένοις	διδομέναις	διδομένοις
	A.	διδομένους	διδομένας	διδόμενα

Note the following:

80

1. The basic stem (δο) is used throughout the declension.
2. The characteristic reduplication is used throughout.
3. The endings are identical to those used in the corresponding forms of verbs of the ω conjugation.

SECOND AORIST ACTIVE PARTICIPLE

		Masculine	Feminine	Neuter
S.	N.	δούς	δοῦσα	δόν
	G.	δόντος	δούσης	δόντος
	D.	δόντι	δούσῃ	δόντι
	A.	δόντα	δοῦσαν	δόν
P.	N.	δόντες	δοῦσαι	δόντα
	G.	δόντων	δουσῶν	δόντων
	D.	δοῦσι	δούσαις	δοῦσι
	A.	δόντας	δούσας	δόντα

SECOND AORIST MIDDLE PARTICIPLE

		Masculine	Feminine	Neuter
S.	N.	δόμενος	δομένη	δόμενον
	G.	δομένου	δομένης	δομένου
	D.	δομένῳ	δομένῃ	δομένῳ
	A.	δόμενον	δομένην	δόμενον
P.	N.	δόμενοι	δόμεναι	δόμενα
	G.	δομένων	δομενῶν	δομένων
	D.	δομένοις	δομέναις	δομένοις
	A.	δομένους	δομένας	δόμενα

These second aorist forms are identical to those of the present participle except that the reduplication has been dropped.

Note: The aorist passive participle occurs only in Ephesians 3:7, where the form δοθείσης (feminine genitive singular) is used.

VIII. INFINITIVES

THE INFINITIVE

Present Active	λύειν
Present Middle and Passive	λύεσθαι
Future Active	λύσειν
Future Middle	λύσεσθαι
Future Passive	λυθήσεσθαι
Aorist Active	λῦσαι
Aorist Middle	λύσασθαι
Aorist Passive	λυθῆναι
Perfect Active	λελυκέναι
Perfect Middle	λελύσθαι
Verb "to be"	εἶναι

Peculiarities

1. All the infinitive forms have endings in ειν or αι.

2. The aorists, though secondary tenses, do not have an augment.

3. The aorist passive, perfect active, and perfect middle forms do not have a recessive accent.

Uses of the Infinitive

1. Supplementary or Complementary — The infinitive completes the thought or action of the verb.

2. Substantive — The infinitive is used in the place of a noun. When so used the infinitive will have the definite article. Thus it is often referred to as "the articular infinitive."

3. Indirect Discourse — This is sometimes expressed by the use of an infinitive with a noun in the accusative case.

THE INFINITIVE

Points of Grammar

1. There is, generally speaking, no distinction of time in the tenses of the infinitive. The aorist is normally used unless there is some reason to indicate continuing or repeated action, in which case the present will generally be used.

2. To indicate a negative with the infinitive the negative particle μή is used.

3. The subject of an infinitive is always in the accusative case.